Carol

I PRAYED FOR PATIENCE

GOD GAVE ME CHILDREN

Enjoy

Linda W. Rondeau

WHAT READERS ARE SAYING ...

about I Prayed for Patience God Gave Me Children

— This book is an immense blessing and very timely in this age of instant information. If you are like me you will want to read this book, keep it close for those moments of weakness and pass it along to your daughters!

— Linda Wood Rondeau brings a lifetime of experience as a parent, grandparent, and social worker to the table in this entertaining, helpful parenting book. A buffet of topics, from teaching kids about money to setting a godly example, will nourish readers' souls.

— Linda Wood Rondeau's stories about the perplexities of parenthood are fresh, moving, and humorous.

— A good devotional for those with children through their teens and even those who have grandchildren.

— Good reminders as I go through this season of motherhood. Also good to know I am not alone in struggling through this life.

— It is a great read with real life applications.

— A good read. The food is so good you want to keep eating more.

— Very enlightening, with quips, quotes, and anecdotes you will want to put up on your refrigerator.

— Written for parents by a parent, this devotional captures both the difficulty as well as the joy of parenthood. Sprinkled with humor, quotes, and nuggets of insight, as well as Bible passages, A meaningful read.

— The author's unique approach illustrates that as we care for our own children and turn to God for help, we learn how God parents and takes care of us as His children.

— A tremendous read, touching and very meaningful. A book every parent should read.

—A parenting book for the supermom in all of us.

— Whether you're looking for an easy-read to spend a little extra time with the Lord after your children have gone to bed, or something to ponder while you're waiting for your little ones to finish practice, this devotional is perfect for any busy mom.

— An amazing ability to partner sweet and fun-loving anecdotes from her own life experience with Scripture and Christian values. I learned a lot and laughed a lot, too!

I PRAYED FOR PATIENCE

GOD GAVE ME CHILDREN
Second Edition

Linda Wood Rondeau

Illustrated by Kevin Scott Collier

PUBLISHING THE POSITIVE

ELK LAKE PUBLISHING INC
Plymouth, Massachusetts

Cover and Interior Design: Derinda Babcock

Editor(s): Dan Hilton, Deb Haggerty

Illustrated by Kevin Scott Collier

Author Represented by the Seymour Agency

PUBLISHED BY: Elk Lake Publishing, Inc., 35 Dogwood Dr., Plymouth, MA 02360, 2019

Library Cataloging Data

Names: Rondeau, Linda Wood (Linda Wood Rondeau)

I Prayed for Patience: God Gave Me Children / Linda Wood Rondeau

162 p. 23cm × 15cm (9in × 6 in.)

Description: A look at parenting from experience and a humorous perspective.

Identifiers: ISBN-13: 978-1-950051-40-3 (trade) | 978-1-950051-41-0 (POD) | 978-1-950051-42-7 (e-book.)

Key Words: Kids, Parents, Child rearing, Family, Discipline, Inspirational, Humor

LCCN: 2019938534 Nonfiction

INTRODUCTION

Parenting is the hardest job in the world. Yet, this is the method God uses to help us understand what being his child means. I hope within these pages you will find a two-step process: first, finding a little help in caring for the child or children God has put in your heart and path. Second, I hope you will discover God's patient love … the joy of being in the palm of his hand.

PART I

PERSEVERE

With all the technological advancements today,
why can't someone invent a child destubbonizer?

A little more persistence, a little more effort,
and what seemed hopeless failure
may turn to glorious success.

Elbert Hubbard
American editor, publisher, and writer (1856-1915)

Late to bed and early to rise makes for a very long day.

He also said, "This is what the kingdom of God is like. A man scatters seed on the ground. Night and day, whether he sleeps or gets up, the seed sprouts and grows, though he does not know how. All by itself the soil produces grain—first the stalk, then the head, then the full kernel in the head. As soon as the grain is ripe, he puts the sickle to it, because the harvest has come." (Mark 4:26–29)

GOD'S SERVER NEVER SHUTS DOWN

"Do you want any help after the baby's born?" my mother asked. She knew. I didn't. I was young and foolhardy.

"No, thank you. I can manage. After all, I've taken care of children my whole life."

How could I have known the difference between caring for someone else's child and my own?

Then they put this eight-pound challenge in my arms. "Congratulations," the doctor said. "Get ready for twenty more years of tired." I suppose he mistook my ashen panic for exhaustion.

As soon as I could get to a phone (in the days before cells), I rethought Mother's kind invitation and relinquished my stalwart independence. "Help! I am scared stiff!"

Wimps beware. Parenting is the ultimate endurance test where wit wins over strength. The job takes more patience than conducting a science experiment, sculpting a masterpiece, or waiting for a fish to bite.

Parenting is hard work.

Whenever I wilted under the heat of day-to-day stress, my own mother would wrap her encouraging arms around me. "Patience, Dear. Rome wasn't built in a day and neither are children."

Therein is the dilemma. Our culture allows us to experience immediate gratification as never before. Technological wonders provide the modern parent with near instantaneous solutions to problems our matriarchal ancestors solved with grit and common sense. Searching *Web MD*, *Women's Day*, *Parenting on a Limited Budget*, or a myriad of search engines, information is but a click away.

Yet, no tome of knowledge can quiet a mother's anxious heart when her child weeps. Nor can a computer wipe away a tear as efficiently as a parent's hug. From the beginning of time, most parents have managed to raise responsible children. The odds are in our favor. Even so, it's nice to know we have help.

More dependable than the fastest wireless connection, God hears our confused cries before they are even uttered. "Do you need my help?"

"Every day in every way," we answer.

INSIGHT

Read James 1:2–7, Ephesians 3:14–21, Romans 5:1–4, Hebrews 6:19, Luke 21:19.

How is parenting, like our faith, a growth process? Do you sometimes feel you can't hold on any longer? What do the above verses teach us about perseverance? How do we apply that as parents? As God's children? Our children do not come with a manual, and each parenting event is peculiar to the individual child. Likewise, our spiritual journey is unique to us. However, we do learn, and we do have a teacher. There will be times our joy in the Lord will be tested, just as children test our patience time and time again. For those inevitable times of doubt, confusion, and frustration, James tells us to seek wisdom from our omnipotent, omniscient, and omnipresent Lord.

PRAYER

Lord, here is my outstretched hand. I pray that you will grab hold of my insecurity, fears, and doubts and lead me on this journey. Help me to remain firm, keeping hope in the finished result.

To finish the journey, one must stay on the road.

These commandments that I give you today are to be upon your hearts. Impress them on your children. Talk about them when you sit at home and when you walk along the road, when you lie down and when you get up. Tie them as symbols on your hands and bind them on your foreheads. Write them on the door frames of your houses and on your gates. (Deuteronomy 6:6–9)

OF PETS AND PERSISTENCE

"That's it! I've had it with this whole thing! He's never going to use it. Why do I even bother?" I moaned after lifting Jimmy off the potty chair for the twentieth time that day. He'd been more interested in the mechanics of the interlocking pieces than performance. My mother laughed. "Parenting is a war of the wills. You have to outlast them. Kids can be persistent, you know."

With the warning, I buckled in for a twenty-year ride on the merry-go-round.

When I hear the word, "persistent," I think of an exasperating, two-pound, orange-and-white terrorist named Duffer, who had set his sights on the glittering balls that adorned our Christmas tree. At first, a stern "No! Duffer!" deterred his intentions—not for long, though. Understanding of the cat's nature, I confidently raised the ornaments a little higher on the tree—out of paws reach. Simple solution—so I thought. Duffer climbed the tree in a formal declaration of war. One morning, I caught him napping in the upper branches, basking in his victory. When the tree toppled over, I settled on a cease-fire agreement. We bought a small fiber-optic tree, hoping time and patience would once again allow us to enjoy our full array of ornaments.

Surrender is easier than continued warfare. It takes less energy to say "Yes," than to put a foot down and utter a stern "No!" Unfortunately, children lack the fundamental capacity to ascertain cause from effect. In a teen's mind, his current cold has little to do with the fact he went outside without a coat.

The child cries for independence, for absolute control of his environment. They will balk at discipline as naturally as they spit out castor oil.

Spiritually, we are much like our stubborn offspring. We expect God to change his laws to suit our desires. When we stumble and fall, we prefer to blame him rather than take accountability for our own poor choices.

God does not give up on us. He delivered his beloved Israel from Egypt and sustained her in the desert. He gave her kings and prophets. When her stubborn heart continued to resist, he sent his only Son, his very representation as an offering and way for reconciliation.

He loves us with that same *everlasting love* (Jeremiah 31:3). He is the Hound of Heaven who relentlessly pursues. His discipline is not meted out with vengeance but delivered with mercy—and infinitesimal patience—a patience that surpasses our hardest resistance.

INSIGHT

Read Acts 9:1–7, Psalm 25:6, Psalm 98:23, Hosea 11:4, Isaiah 45:17.

In Acts 9, the King James Version adds a phrase: "It is hard for thee to kick against the pricks." Another translation uses the word goads. What do you think this means? Paul persecuted the Christians because he believed they posed a danger to Judaism. How did his Damascus Road experience change the direction of his life? How has God changed a direction in your life because of his persistent chase for your heart?

PRAYER

Hound of Heaven, thank you for your pursuit. I now surrender to you those stubborn streaks that have kept me from knowing the fullness of your unrelenting love.

If at first you don't succeed, take a bubble bath.

For the Lord gives wisdom; and from his mouth come knowledge and understanding. He holds success in store for the upright, he is a shield to those whose walk is blameless, for he guards the course of the just and protects the way of his faithful ones. Then you will understand what is right and just and fair—every good path. For wisdom will enter your heart, and knowledge will be pleasant to your soul. Discretion will protect you, and understanding will guard you. (Proverbs 2:6–11)

PATIENT WISDOM

A parent's intelligence is directly proportionate to the age of her child.

Any three-year-old knows that Mom and Dad are Information Central or that they have the power to make his favorite television show appear on demand, even if streaming is not available. Mommy knows how many stars are in the sky, why the sun always shines in the morning, and why we can only see the moon at night. "Why is the grass green? Why is the sky blue? Why do you have to wash the dishes now? Why does the baby get to wet in his diaper?" One after another, the questions are harpooned throughout the day. The child is confident that his parents always know the answer.

Teenagers, on the other hand, are convinced that their parents' brains are made of oatmeal. Parents are the *last* people on earth to whom they would go for information—at least not until they've checked all their social media sites. They distrust their parents' opinions in most arenas. Only when their need exceeds their disbelief will they surrender their doubts and seek a word of wisdom from Dear Old Mom and Dad.

Sometimes our children's problems are beyond humankind's conventional wisdom. We look in every direction for solutions. Counselors blame parents, and doctors shake their heads in defeat. Lawyers cry for financial compensation, asking the court to determine who's to blame. God our Father knows the future as well as the present. He who gives all things abundantly stands ready to intercede.

Noah was clueless when God told him to build an ark. "An ark? You want it how big? You're kidding! Rain? What's that?" God took Noah through the process step by step.

Moses led a million Hebrews and their families across a wasteland. God gave him Aaron and Miriam as helpers. Joshua walked around the city of Jericho seven times as commanded, and then the walls came down.

What seems like foolishness to us is God's wisdom at work. When Kiley must be rushed to the hospital for a ruptured appendix, we place our trust in a very human and imperfect physician. How much more can we trust our children's insolvable problems in the hands of a perfect God?

I remember the sensation of horror when touring a coal mine. The guide warned us we'd be in total darkness for about a minute. That did very little to defuse the complete disorientation of the experience. Even in the darkest night, one can at least see shadows. In that mine, there was nothing. We were completely dependent upon our guide.

The Christian experiencing the worst darkness is not without a guide ... a perfect Shepherd who knows the way before us. All we need do is grab his hand. He will give us instruction when we need to turn left or right or stay straight on our course.

INSIGHT

Read 1 Kings 3:9; 4:29–34 and Proverbs 3:5, 6.

What did Solomon ask of God when he took the throne? How did God answer? Why is it so hard to not lean on our understanding? What is it about our human nature that makes trust so difficult? What about your own personal experiences? Why do you suppose you have found it difficult to trust the Lord at times? We have a sure anchor, and we can trust he will keep us safe during the storm ... if we put our trust in him.

PRAYER

Lord, I know in my head that you are the way, the truth, and the life. I know that you are all powerful, all knowing, and all present. Yet, there are times I want to solve my problems within my own scope of knowledge. Strange that I am even more resistant when the answers seem beyond my grasp. Remind me, Lord, of your love, compassion, and mercy. Reassure me that your ways are always the right ways. Develop in me a spirit that will run to you with all of life's quagmires.

I multitask my worries. I pace during the spin cycle.

Do not be anxious about anything, but in everything, by prayer and petition, with thanksgiving, present your requests to God. And the peace of God, which transcends all understanding, will guard your hearts and your minds in Christ Jesus. (Philippians 4:6–7)

PATIENT PRAYING

I whooped and hollered with more enthusiasm than a teen at a rock concert. Among all the parents present at that basic training graduation, I was among the most grateful.

For many young people, the first few months out of college can be a difficult transition. Some are fortunate enough to know they will attend graduate school or find employment in their field of education. Jim was one of the uncertain multitudes. When he announced his decision to enter the Army, mouths went agape.

Jim could have penned the book, *The Art of Passive Resistance for Children*. Like the mountain, he would not be moved. He was God's answer to a prayer for patience. With more skill than an X-Box Samurai, he wielded his defiant sword against every discipline technique I tried.

My first mistake was to own blame—to convince myself that Jim's non-compliant nature was my fault. Because I believed I was the cause, I took every right turn available. One does not make forward progress by taking so many detours. Against all my Herculean efforts, Jim's passivity deepened with each passing year.

Like fighting fire with fire, every parental "trick" was out maneuvered. I took away his allowance—he managed with less. I took away his television—he read comics. Warnings railed into purposefully deafened ears. All our exaggerated attempts only served to feed his amusement.

Had I lost the war?

God jolted my memory. "If any of you lacks wisdom, he should ask God, who gives generously to all without finding fault, and it will be given to him" (James 1:5). In desperation, I finally turned to God, pleading for his wisdom instead of relying on my own inadequate strength.

Then the epiphany came.

God had designed Jim, doggedness included. Someday that hard-core resistance would become steadfastness. Annoying stubbornness would move him to conviction and that constant rebelliousness would evolve into courage—according to God's timetable, not mine. From then on, I sought to nurture his independence proactively instead of waging war against it. We both survived his growing up, and he emerged a man of honor.

I watched my stubborn soldier move methodically through his drills, secretly beaming with pride and assured that God was completing the good work he started.

INSIGHT

Read Philippians 1:3–9, 1 Corinthians 1:4–9, Colossians 1:3–14, 2 Thessalonians 1:3–4.

These verses give us insight into Paul's desire for his flock. In what way does he sound like a concerned father? Have you come to a place where you worry all the effort you've placed into your child's upbringing might be for naught? Do you worry over personality traits or bad influences? Ultimately, Paul surrenders his concern with confidence that God would continue to work in this church even after his death. We can be confident that God loves the children we care for as much as we do … even more so. We can be confident that the good seed we've planted in them will eventually take root. Perhaps not in the way we envisioned, but in God's good time and God's good way. Never stop praying.

PRAYER

Lord, I can't count the number of times I've been willful, messed up, made wrong choices, and detoured from the life you had planned for me. For these times, I repent. Yet, you have promised to complete the good work you have started in me. Help me to learn from those errors, to rest in the confidence that you can still make all things good for my sake. Let me forget about yesterday and hold your hand as we face tomorrow together.

If children hired parents, most of us would be standing in the unemployment line.

The Spirit you received does not make you slaves, so that you live in fear again; rather, the Spirit you received brought about your adoption to sonship. And by him we cry, "Abba, Father." (Romans 8:15)

JUST LIKE MY DADDY

The courtroom was silent, waiting for the judge to make a decision—a decision to determine not only where little Joshua would live, but also what his name would be.

Not able to have children of their own, *Lisa and David adopted five children through the foster care system. Each addition to the family was considered a blessing—especially so with Joshua. Having already adopted two others, Joshua was next to be officially made their son. When the agency called to inform them Joshua could now be theirs, Lisa and David were thrilled and looked forward to this day in court.

The judge motioned four-year old Joshua to approach the bench. From his austere height, the magistrate pointed to various people in the courtroom one by one. Each time, Joshua was asked "Who is this?"

"My brothers, my uncles, my mother." All those who had cared and loved Joshua over the past three years.

Then the judge's attention focused on David, who lifted Joshua into his arms, allowing the child to see the judge at eye level. "And who is this man holding you?"

Joshua's eyes widened. He took his little hand and touched his father's face as he squealed in delight, "THAT'S MY DADDY!"

The judge, assured of Joshua's placement in a loving family, told Lisa and David that Joshua was now their legal son by order of the court. Then the judge asked Joshua, "Do you know what your new name is?"

Joshua hugged his father and blurted with excitement, "Joshua David, just like my daddy!"

Sad are the indictments against Israel's kings who "walked in the ways of their fathers" to commit vile acts of murder and idolatry. Sadder still are the descriptions of those sons who choose evil over the godly example of their fathers. David was revered as a man after God's heart because he cherished the relationship he had with his heavenly father more than any earthly treasure.

When he sinned, he could not rest until his spirit was one again with the God he adored.

Is it any wonder David was described as a "man after God's own heart?"

When we received Christ, God adopted us into his family. He holds us in his arms so we can touch his face. We are privileged to call him "Daddy, God."

He asks us to be holy as he is holy. He asks us to look inside our hearts and say, "I want to be just like you."

*not their real names

INSIGHT

Read Psalm 27:10, John 1:12, 2 Corinthians 6:18, Galatians 4:3–7.

What is the difference between a slave and son? How does the realization that we are God's child change your view regarding your relationship with him? God has not called us to be his slaves but his children.

PRAYER

Thank you, Lord, for the sacrifice you gave to make me your child. Help me to live like your daughter. Though I don't comprehend, remind me that I am precious in your sight. You have made me an heir together with your son, Jesus Christ.

PART II

TEACH

How can I teach my children to drive when I can't even parallel park?

Education is what survives
when what has been learned has been forgotten.
B.F. Sinner, psychologist (1904-1990)

Life is a smorgasbord. The trick is getting to the dessert table before our plates are too full.

The heart is deceitful above all things and beyond cure. Who can understand it? (Jeremiah 17:9)

DOUBLE CHOCOLATE TROUBLE

How then do we weak and feeble-minded grownups teach responsibility to impetuous youngsters?

Melissa, the mother of three highly spirited and independent preschoolers, has learned the value of avoiding open-ended questions. Instead of "What do you want for breakfast?" She asks, "Do you want pancakes or French toast?"

The open-ended question "What do you want for breakfast?" may be honestly answered with "Chocolate cake!" The child fully expects to see the frosted delight delivered at his command.

"No! You can't have chocolate cake. That's not a breakfast food!"

"But I want it."

"I said no!"

The screech that erupts now turns breakfast into a Maalox Moment. If there are multiple children, bedlam follows, for now they all want the chocolate cake. They are either sent to their rooms, or more is the pity—they are served the chocolate cake.

By giving children carefully guided choices, the parent is assured of a positive outcome. We limit our children's choices because we love them. We understand their bent for chocolate and the harm too much chocolate will inflict.

We do all we can to nurture good decision-making skills in our children, yet as adults, we fail to heed the warnings that are blatantly in front of us. We see the sign. *Thin ice*. Yet, we keep on walking and wonder why we find ourselves submerged in frigid waters.

When Nehemiah, commissioned for the rebuilding of Jerusalem, studied the law and the rebellious history of his people, he marveled at God's compassion. "In all that has happened to us, you have remained righteous; you have acted faithfully, while we acted wickedly." (Nehemiah 9:33). God had orchestrated the seventy years of captivity in order to preserve the Jewish nation ... for from this house of David, the King of Kings would be born.

God foreknew the right time Christ would come into the world and save his chosen people so that the world, through him, would be blessed. The Lord hedged Israel into limited choices … not out of vengeance … but to protect.

We often hound God for the chocolate cake of comfort, wealth, or fame. Instead, he fashions our choices to preserve our relationship with him.

The Bible tells us that our hearts are naturally deceitful, and our own wills will lead us astray. Is there hope? Yes, there is great hope for the believer. The Father reveals the best of all choices, and those who trust in God will prosper.

INSIGHT

Read Psalm 1, 1 Kings 8:36, Psalm 86:11, Psalm 143:10, Lamentations 3:40, Psalm 27:11, Psalm 25:9, Psalm 119:15, Psalm 143:8, Psalm 32:8.

Psalm 1 shows two different routes and their consequences. Describe the characteristics of each way. What makes the difference? The remaining verses demonstrate how the Lord teaches us through careful guidance. List some of the ways the Psalmists praise the Lord for his teaching. How do they respond to God's teaching? Has the Lord ever hemmed you in, limited your choices, and then showed you a better way?

PRAYER

Lord, as a loving father, you want what is best for me and for our relationship. Teach me what is the right way and give me the strength to follow. Hedge me in from above and around so that the steps I take are those you have designed for me.

Mama said there'd be days like this, but she didn't say there'd be so many.

My message and my preaching were not with wise and persuasive words, but with a demonstration of the Spirit's power, so that your faith might not rest on human wisdom, but on God's power. (1 Corinthians 2:4)

THE CHOICE TO FAIL

"I don't care what you pick but pick something!"

*Kaitlin's eleven-year-old son had become one with the couch. She could barely distinguish where his body ended and the cushions began. Mr. Negativity booed every suggestion she made. Finally, she passed a mandate. He'd have to find some sort of activity. His choice—but at least something.

He tried a variety of instruments from horns to reeds only to discover not only a dearth of talent but a complete lack of interest. Thankfully, the drums fell into the latter category. She suggested perhaps music was not his thing. He tried track, dropping out in mid-season when he gasped for breath just doing the fifty-yard dash. He played hockey for one season but tired of sitting on the bench because the coach only played the better skaters.

The list of failed attempts grew—sometimes because of poor effort and sometimes because adults failed to encourage him. Then he went out for the swim team. He never became a fast swimmer, but as his strength increased, so did his endurance. He became a competent, long-distance swimmer, usually placing well enough to earn his team a few points. He advanced his skills to become a lifeguard and camp counselor. "He's the best swimming instructor they've got," one woman remarked. He learned that failure was merely the opportunity to try something else.

Our Father knows we are not the brightest kids on the block, yet he still gives us the power of free will. After a few blunders, we eventually learn to place our trust in his perfect wisdom. We may even come to the realization that God actually knows what is best for us and seek his will before making life-changing decisions.

The Abraham who was willing to sacrifice Isaac was not the same Abram who left Ur of the Chaldeans. As he grew in the knowledge of God's ways, he learned to wait on God, knowing that the Lord would bring to pass what he had promised.

Failure is a teacher that forces us to evaluate and redirect. We grow by falling down, standing up, and trying again. But, when we fail, God does not leave us crying face down in the dirt. He puts his loving arms around us, picks us up, and dusts us off. He may send us right back into the game or encourage us to try something different. With each attempt, we learn to trust him a little more.

*not her real name

INSIGHT

Read Luke 5:1–11, Kings 8:33–34, Galatians 2:1–9, Acts 2:37–38.

The fishermen and Paul struggled to achieve their goals. How were their failures to ultimately lead to success? Have you ever cast your net after repeated failures on the encouragement of someone you admired, and then finally succeeded? Peter and his partners and tried and tried and tried again. What made the difference this time? Are there times when failure moves us into a different direction before we achieve success?

PRAYER

Lord, help me not to be quick to give up. Yet, help me to examine my failure to determine what might be the cause. Did I sin? Did I cast my net in the wrong place? Did I deter from your instruction? Have I been trying to do things on my own? Give me wisdom to come to you when things are not going well.

A penny saved is a penny earned. That's before taxes.

In him, we have redemption through his blood, the forgiveness of sins, in accordance with the riches of God's grace that he lavished on us. With all wisdom and understanding, And you also were included in Christ when you heard the message of truth, the gospel of your salvation. When you believed, you were marked in him with a seal, the promised Holy Spirit, who is a deposit guaranteeing our inheritance until the redemption of those who are God's. also having believed, you were marked in him with a seal, the promised Holy Spirit, who is a deposit guaranteeing our inheritance until the redemption of those who are God's possession—to the praise of his glory. (Ephesians 1: 7–8, 13b–14)

NUGGETS OF GRACE

Experts still cannot agree on the value of giving a child an allowance. If an allowance were granted, then a parent must determine the parameters upon how the practice would be implemented. What expectations should be attached to the privilege?

Our children became adept at manipulating allowances to their favor. They abandoned non-paid chores to perform the more lucrative tasks. As we muddled through allowance negotiations, I stocked up on aspirin.

Then, they decided to become paper delivery people. Proponents advocated this endeavor would teach children how to run their own business. Who substituted for the young entrepreneur when he was in bed with the flu? I trudged through the three-foot snowdrifts proud my children were learning the value of money. Who was I kidding? When customers failed to make their payments on time, The First National Bank of Rondeau doled out compassionate loans. I needed a ledger to keep track of *my* money going in and out of *their* business!

Then along came part-time jobs. Our calendar looked like the arrival and departure schedules at O'Hare. I never knew how many plates to set for dinner. To cope with uncertainties, we invented the phrase *fend for yourself supper*. When the children inquired as to the evening's menu, I would respond with a frustrated, "Fend for yourself!" I kept the cupboards stocked with easy-to-prepare meals. Of course, who had to transport all the workers to their jobs? The grocery bill skyrocketed while the gas bill tripled.

I wondered. Had all the efforts done any good? Did I teach them anything at all?

Only time would tell. In the meantime, I would continue to at least try to demonstrate fiscal responsibility. Or perhaps the lesson is not in methodology but in the intent. Mom and Dad may be helpers, but the Lord is the One who supplies.

I thought of the widow who had reached the end of her sustenance. Like beauty and power, we tend to see our lack rather than our abundance. We feel trapped in our need. Such was the experience of this widow mentioned in 2 Kings. She feared losing her sons to slavery, a fate far worse than starvation.

With no other options, she turned to the prophet. Though what he suggested seemed absurd, she obeyed. God multiplied her current resources until the creditors' demands were met, and she was told to live on what remained. She was content.

The Bible has much to say about how we should acquire and utilize our possessions. However, two basic principles come to mind. God is our supplier, and he expects us to be content with what he provides. Secondly, no matter how many or how few material gifts we give our children, the greatest treasures we can bestow are daily nuggets of God's truths. His economy knows neither depression nor recession, and his vaults are inexhaustible.

INSIGHT

Read Mathew 6:25–34, Philippians 4:11–13.

What advice does Paul give to help overcome anxiety concerning our temporal life? Jesus reminds us of our value to the father. What are several reasons why we should not worry? It is human nature to be concerned about our finances, our household, and our temporal comforts. When these are threatened, our impulse is to become anxious. We can counteract those fears with the knowledge that God cares for us even more than the sparrow and the lilies of the field.

PRAYER

Father, when times of financial distress come my way, help me to remember my value in your eyes. Fill me with reassurance that you are my Provider and teach me to me content with whatever you have given me.

If life were simple, there'd be no geometry.

Teach me, LORD, the way of your decrees, that I may follow it to the end. Give me understanding, so that I may keep your law and obey it with all my heart. (Psalm 119:33–34)

A TEENAGED ROBIN HOOD

*Marla knew something was wrong when her teenager came home from school, dropped his books with a thunderous thud on the table, wolfed down four peanut butter sandwiches without taking a breath, then asked, "What's for dinner?" He was still a growing boy, but this inability to satiate was abnormal even for a body-builder.

"What did you have for lunch?" she asked.

He scowled, muttered something about the inedible cafeteria food, collected his books, and hiked up the stairs taking three at a time. His hurried demeanor raised even more suspicions. She trotted up after him.

"Something's not right here." Marla gave him that no-more-foolishness-I-want-the-truth-now kind of stare. It worked.

"You know how I've been supporting this kid through the Save-the-Children Foundation."

"Yes. And we're very proud of you."

"Well, I've been using my lunch money you give me every week."

On one hand, Marla took pride in her son's good heart. On the other hand, The Robin Hood Excuse didn't quite cut it. The truth was, he had misappropriated funds. *Her funds.* She was the one supporting the orphan, not him. He'd make up for his temporary deprivation by emptying out the cupboards after school.

"Look. That money was given to you for a distinct purpose. Using it for other reasons without permission is tantamount to stealing."

At first, her son merely stared back blankly as if stunned he was being scolded instead of praised. Finally, truth sank in. The subtlety of the offense was understood. While his motives were pure, his execution was faulty. Since he wanted to help the poor, Marla found extra jobs for him to do. That way, he learned the meaning of true sacrifice.

Sin likes to hide in the pretense of good. White and black blend into shades of gray, and right becomes more difficult to distinguish. Paul said, "So

I find this law at work. When I want to do good, evil is right there with me …What a wretched man I am! Who will rescue me from this body of death? Thanks be to God—through Jesus Christ our Lord!" (Romans 7:21, 24–25).

Obedience and discernment are the natural outgrowths from an intimate relationship with Jesus. As we draw nearer to him, his truth enlightens us. We avoid the subtle sin, not because we fear punishment, but because we understand the value of goodness.

*not the real name

INSIGHT

Read Proverbs 2:1–6; 21:2, Matthew 12:1–8, Psalm 139:23–24.

How do we achieve discernment from what may seem right but may not be pleasing in God's eyes? God has given us the Holy Spirit to teach us what God's ways are as opposed to the world's. Have you ever followed a direction which seemed right … from pure motives … but that turned out to be the world's ways and not God's? What helped you to see the difference?

PRAYER

Lord, teach me to discern between what seems good to men and what is pleasing in your sight.

Watch where you step. Little ones are right behind you.

If you point these things out to the brother and sisters, you will be a good minister of Christ Jesus, nourished on the truths of the faith and of the good teaching that you have followed. Have nothing to do with godless myths and old wives' tales; rather, train yourself to be godly. For physical training is of some value, but godliness has value for all things, holding promise for both the present life and the life to come. (1 Timothy 4:6–8)

A LIFELONG PURSUIT

"Back, Sheba, back!" The lion tamer snaps the whip, and the fierce lioness retreats to the cage. With one click, the mighty beast is subdued. Why isn't parenting that simple? Why won't our children respond with the snap of the whip and heel at our command?

We awake from our fantasy with the crash of the milk carton on the floor. "Oops, sorry." Jackson tries to sneak out the door with the white liquid oozing all over the linoleum.

"You get right back in here, young man, and clean that mess up this instant!"

"Oh, Mom!"

"You heard me!"

"But, Micah's waiting!"

"Let him wait."

Meanwhile, the liquid is congealing on the floor.

"But we'll be late."

"The more you argue, the later you'll be."

"Aww, Mom!"

Reluctantly, Jackson cleans up the mess—most likely not a professional offering. He runs off for his rendezvous with Micah while his mother's slippers stick to the floor. She wonders *will he ever learn?*

During the training years, a child fails many times before he achieves competency. Webster defines the word "train" as follows: "To form by instruction, discipline, or drill, to teach so as to make fit, qualified, or proficient."

In Matthew 10, we read how Jesus sent his disciples out two by two. He gave them instructions; however, the learning would be on-the-job training. Much like parenting. This assignment would be a precursor of what was to come after Jesus's death so that when they received the Great Commission, Matthew 28, they would have had some experience to draw upon.

Likewise, God teaches us from life experiences.

There will come a day when our training efforts will yield good fruit in our children. The evidence of our instruction will be revealed during their later years and in future generations to come. Like profits from a mutual fund, the yield takes time.

Likewise, God has confidence in our conclusion. He fits and equips us for the work he has destined. Immediate results are rare. Just as the delicate orchid takes years to bloom, God's pruning in our lives takes decades. There will come a time when he will welcome us into his presence and say with great parental pleasure, "Well done, my child!"

INSIGHT

Read Ephesians 2:1–10, Numbers 27:18–23, Deuteronomy 32:9–14, Jeremiah 16:21, Mark 2:13, Ezekiel 36:26.

Moses instructed Joshua, and then Joshua became the leader after Moses died. The Lord himself will instruct his child in the way he wants his child to go. Though Paul had the best education available, taught in all aspects of the law, the Lord caused him to wait many years before beginning his ministry as he relearned how Jesus was the embodiment of the law. Our spiritual journey is a process, beginning when we accept Christ's work on the cross, confess our sins, and consciously desire to let him rule in our hearts. Some things change immediately. Some change is a metamorphosis. Some change is difficult because we are reluctant to let go of a lifestyle choice or control over an area of our lives. God has designed our journey with him, his desire that we complete the good work he has ordained for us. As you examine your own life, where have you seen change? Was it spontaneous or did the change evolve over time? Is there an area in your life you have yet to surrender to God's chisel? Do so now.

PRAYER

Lord, self-reflection is hurtful. I ache with the truth you reveal to me. I want to be the person you want me to be. Lord, I give you my past, present, and future for only you will make all things beautiful in your time.

PART III

LEAD

If I'm queen of my castle, why am I the one folding clothes?

A real leader faces the music,
even when he doesn't like the tune
Anonymous

He who rules with an iron fist
breaks a lot of furniture.

To fear the LORD is to hate evil; I hate pride and arrogance, evil behavior and perverse speech. Counsel and sound judgment are mine; I have insight. I have power. By me kings reign and rulers issue decrees that are just; by me princes govern, and nobles—all who rule on earth. (Proverbs 8:13–16)

THE POWER OF ONE

My coworker, Cherrie, and I were commiserating about the tribulations of raising teenagers. In mid-discourse, she received a phone call from her sixteen-year-old. I overheard Cherrie's loud objections as she argued with her daughter. "No, you most certainly cannot go with your boyfriend on an overnight trip." Apparently, Cherrie's daughter raised objections of her own. Finally, Cherrie ended the debate. "I am the Queen. Fear me!"

Parents often forget the power they possess by being older, wiser, and stronger than their children. They hold the purse strings. When our little princes and princesses are born, we, the royalty, legislate, judge, and execute the law. The home is not a democracy—it is a benign monarchy.

My children gave me a plaque that sports the truism "If Mama ain't happy, ain't nobody happy." It was prominently displayed as a reminder: "Don't mess with the queen."

As a social worker, I frequently encouraged parents to establish benevolent authority in the home. Tyrannical parents may produce children who revolt. However, when parents make little effort to reign, children run amuck.

A child's perception of authority is well established even before the age of six. How authority is imputed in the home will have a lasting impact on our progeny. God told Moses … "for, I, the Lord your God, am a jealous God, punishing the children for the sin of the fathers to the third and fourth generation of those who hate me, but showing love to a thousand generations of those who love me and keep my commandments" (Exodus 20:5). Establishing a God-like authority is for the good of our children and our children's children.

God's authority is never rendered arbitrarily. His edicts have purpose and direction, and we are the better when we adhere to them.

Webster defines authority as a *convincing force*. A God-like authority is final. When God speaks, the tidal waves recede and peace is restored.

Throughout the Bible, God ended his instructions with the only qualification necessary to establish his authority, "I am the Lord, your God."

We do well to listen.

INSIGHT

Read Deuteronomy 4:32–39, Psalms 9:7–8, Proverbs 16:9, Isaiah 44:24–25, Revelation 22:13.

Throughout Scripture God establishes his authority. Yet, he is patient with us as his children when we are pouting, demanding, and questioning. He gently reminds us, perhaps sometimes more sternly than at other times, "I am the Lord. There is no other" (Isa. 45:5). Have you ever had an experience where God pinned your ears back or brought you up short to remind you that he is the Lord?

PRAYER

Lord, forgive my whining and demands. Remind me that you are in control of all our circumstances. Remind me when you hedge me in or detour my selfish requests, you do so for my ultimate benefit. You are the beginning and the end. You know the outcome of this difficulty. Help me to surrender to your sovereignty and to trust in your great love for me.

If you want to know what your child will be like in twenty years, look in the mirror.

And have you completely forgotten this word of encouragement that addresses you as a father addresses his son? It says, "My son, do not make light of the Lord's discipline, and do not lose heart when he rebukes you, because the Lord disciplines the one he loves, and he chastens everyone he accepts as a son." Moreover, we have all had human fathers who disciplined us and we respected them for it. How much more should we submit to the Father of spirits and live! They disciplined us for a little while as they thought best; but God disciplines us for our good, in order that we may share in his holiness. (Hebrews 12:5b–6, 9-10)

THESE BOOTS WERE MADE FOR WALKING

Clop! Clop!

The noise wasn't horses. His two-year-old son was clopping through the house in his father's size twelve army boots. The child loved shoes of all kinds, but he especially loved his father's. Whenever he donned them, he became a two-foot soldier trekking after the enemy.

His father laughed. "Guess I should be careful where I take those boots."

Like Mary's little lamb, wherever we go, our children are sure to follow. Parents lead by example, and a child's moral legacy will be influenced more by what the parent does than any other influence. Human services counselors call this "parent modeling."

If we want to know what we look like to our children, we need only listen to them at play. They mimic us with more accuracy than any actor. What do our children hear? Do they hear praise or gossip? Do they hear singing or screaming? Do they hear prayers or curses? Do they hear whining or confidence?

What do they see? Do they see self-control or anger? Do they see faith in action or anxious wanderings? Do they see generosity or miserliness?

Because we love God, we want to be more like him. He has given us his Son for an example. As we pattern our lives after God's precepts, we will not be ashamed in our daily walk. We will be real soldiers in God's army, not wearing clumsy shoes. Our walk will testify to what we believe. Our speech will reflect what is in our hearts.

INSIGHT

Read 2 Corinthians 4:1–6, Colossians 1:15–20, John 13:1–10.

How does Christ "set an example" for his disciples? How does knowing that Christ is the image of God enhance our relationship with him? How do we know Christ is the physical image of God on Earth? What divine qualities does Paul list to prove this claim that Christ is the image of the invisible God? Since we have his example, how does this impact our material life? The Bible gives us everything we need to know to be like Christ. If he is our brother, and he is God, then he is able to empower us to be more like him.

PRAYER

Lord, I want to be more like you. I want to be an example for my children and to be a reflection of the light you have put within me. I need you to show me … to fashion my innermost being so that my comings and goings evidence the faith I have in you.

Why is it that children can hear
the Good Humor truck a mile away
but turn deaf when they're asked to do the dishes?

Search me, God, and know my heart; test me and know my anxious thoughts.

See if there is any offensive way in me, and lead me in the way everlasting.

(Psalms 139:23-24)

MY SHEEP KNOW MY VOICE

"I know the government says I'm not supposed to spank my son," she said.

While performing New York State child protective investigations, I often had to explain to parents the differences between disciplined spanking and physical abuse. At that time, New York State permitted spanking a child if done appropriately. I spent the better part of an hour explaining the legal parameters of spanking as well as alternative methods of discipline.

My client turned to her son while pointing at me. "Did you hear that? Mrs. Rondeau said I could crack you one." *Shirley was not abusive in her dispensing of punishment, but she failed to grasp the intent of the law.

Shirley is not alone in the misguided interpretation of the adage: "Spare the rod, and spoil the child," a paraphrase of Proverbs 13:24. "Whoever spares the rod hates their children, but the one who loves their children is careful to discipline them." All too often, those who spout the verse tend to use the Scripture as a means to enforce compliance rather than lead the child in the right direction.

The shepherd's staff, or rod, was a hooked piece of wood. It was also a symbol of royalty. When monarchy was established in Israel, the scepter was modeled after the shepherd's crook to remind the king to lead the people as a shepherd tended his flock.

Shepherds did not beat their sheep. Sheep were docile, tame creatures that needed only gentle prodding. Shepherds also used the rod to drive away predators. The crook at the end of the rod allowed the shepherd to gently pull back a wandering lamb. The sheep knew the shepherd and followed him wherever he led. As long as they could see the shepherd's staff, the sheep knew they were safe.

Paul said, " Godly sorrow brings repentance that leads to salvation and leaves no regret, but worldly sorrow brings death." (2 Corinthians 7:10).

Jesus is the Good Shepherd. When we walk closely with him, we recognize his voice as the docile sheep of the pasture knew their shepherd's voice. God disciplines us because he loves us. Sometimes he nudges gently. Other times, he takes a symbolic two-by-four and knocks us off our feet. Whatever he must do to keep us safely in the fold, he will do.

INSIGHT

Read John 13:14–16, John 21:17, 1 Peter 5:2, Psalm 23, Exodus 18:14–27, Isaiah 40:11.

How is Jesus like a good Shepherd? What do you think he means when he says, "My sheep know my voice?" What "stranger's voice" might try to lead the sheep astray? Jesus tells Peter to "feed my sheep." What does Peter advise to other Christians? Moses was overwhelmed with managing the vast numbers of Israelites. What advice did his father-in-law give him? Remember that Moses was a shepherd during his exile years from Egypt. How can we apply Jethro's advice to parenting?

PRAYER

Lord, attune my ears to hear only your voice. Give me a trusting spirit that will follow you. Help me to understand what it means to shepherd my children. Give me wisdom to discipline as you discipline me … with love and knowledge of what is good. I am glad you lead me in the way everlasting.

Your legacy is seen in what adorns your refrigerator door.

The fear of the Lord is the beginning of wisdom,
and knowledge of the Holy One is understanding.
(Proverbs 9:10)

A ROYAL LEGACY

My children from my first marriage were close to my second mother-in-law, Kathryn—grandchildren by way of inheritance and not of natural birth. Her biological grandchildren moved from the area soon after their father died. Though this part of the family maintained an intermittent connection, her love for them bridged the barriers of distance and change.

Since we lived in close proximity, we were blessed with the fullness of her. Though my children were given to her by unusual means, she received them as her own, deeply committed to her part in their lives. Her legacy of love provided an example for me as I, too, became the proud grandmother of beautiful adopted children.

Ruth was a Moabite, married to a Hebrew, and was a woman with less than a desirable heritage. Tragedy struck, not only taking the life of Ruth's husband, but her brother-in-law and father-in-law as well. When Ruth's mother-in-law Naomi, grief stricken, announced she would return to her ancestral home, she told her daughters-in-law to go to their family homes.

Ruth refused to leave her mother-in-law. Israel was Naomi's home but a foreign land to Ruth. Because of her great love toward the mother of her husband, Ruth clung to Naomi's God and was the benefactor of Naomi's faith. God rewarded Ruth's courage. Her strength and faith in dire circumstances was brought to the attention of Naomi's kinsman, Boaz, providing us with one of the greatest love stories of the Bible. Ruth's legacy reached through the ages as she became the great-grandmother to King David and one of the few women mentioned in the genealogies of Christ. Through inclusion, her legacy led to the fulfillment of God's redemptive plan.

The believer is grafted into God's royal family thus changing our inheritance forever regardless of our original roots. God weaves a tapestry of Divine influence for our descendants.

He changes the unnatural into the natural and makes us joint heirs with his son, Christ Jesus, giving us the full rights of Heaven—a royal and eternal legacy.

INSIGHT

Read 1 Peter 1:3–5, 1 Peter 5:4, Hebrews 3:6, Psalm 47:4, Romans 8:17, Colossians 3:24.

What are we given? In whom is our hope? What do we inherit? Where is our inheritance kept? Knowing that our eternal God has kept our eternal inheritance gives us a sense of permanency in contrast to the temporary conditions of life. Lineage was important for status in Biblical times. Why is it significant that we are in God's house? God promises to keep us until that day we receive our inheritance. Our legacy cannot be measured in monetary wealth. It is intangible but none the less precious.

PRAYER

Father God, remind me of your ever-present self and of the hope you have given us through your son, Jesus Christ. When circumstances and suffering would make us doubt our firm relationship with you, help us remember the hope to which we are called. May our lives in turn be a legacy for those who follow.

Sometimes we lead only because
everyone else is behind us.

Who is wise? Let them realize these things. Who is discerning? Let them understand. The ways of the Lord are right; the righteous walk in them, but the rebellious stumble in them. (Hosea 14:9)

FOLLOW WHICH LEADER?

We are often guilty of inaction because we don't know what action to take. We want someone to tell us exactly what to do. We want a recipe for parenting that makes sense. We find it easier to follow someone else's prescription than to make our own diagnosis. I'm reminded of the old television series, *Home Improvement*, starring Tim Allen … a befuddled dad and cable television repair show host. When Tim "The Tool Man" Taylor faced a seemingly unsolvable puzzle, he'd wander over to the backyard and have a little talk with his ever faceless but always wise neighbor, Wilson.

We all want a neighbor like Wilson, full of wisdom just when we need it.

The story is told of a man who fell into a hole and couldn't climb out. His doctor went by. "Mighty deep hole you're in," he said. He scribbled a prescription and threw it in to him, then left.

Later, his teacher came by and recited many theories about deep holes. "You should avoid them," he said. And he left.

Next, his pastor came by. "I see you are in a deep hole, son. I'll be sure to pray for you," he said and left.

The poor man thought he'd surely starve to death. Finally, a friend came by and jumped in the hole with him. The man was aghast. "What did you do that for?" he asked his friend. "Now there are two of us stuck down here."

"You don't understand," said the friend. "I've been in this hole before, and I know the way out. Follow me."

Perhaps this is the key to parenting … helping our children avoid the pitfalls we fell into. And if they should fall into similar snares, rather than condemnation and lectures, letting them know … we've been there, or someplace similar, and survived with God's help. Equipped with wisdom from on high, we may be able to show them solutions to what seems to them insurmountable problems.

Jesus knows the path we follow. Those of us without a next-door over-the-fence psychologist and who are left to muddle through can take heart. Jesus not only knows the way out, he takes us by the hand and leads us home.

INSIGHT

Read Hebrews 4:15, Numbers 11:4–15, Nehemiah 5:1–18, Joshua 1:5–7, 2 Samuel 23:3–4, 1 Chronicles 18:14, Hosea 12:13, 1 Thessalonians 2:1–16. Who is our high priest … our leader? How should we approach the throne of God? What does the writer of Hebrews mean "To hold firmly to the faith we profess? Does he suggest we should never doubt? Of course not. However, when doubts come, and they will, we are assured that Christ, who has been where we are and has gone ahead, comes by our side to lead us on. This is our confidence. Moses and Nehemiah are examples of leadership struggles. How did Moses handle the complaints of his charge? What advice was Joshua given? Sometimes, a leader must take the complaint to the Lord and ask him for guidance. How did Moses, Joshua, and Nehemiah model an example of leadership? What advice can we glean from Paul's letter to the Thessalonians? How did they lead?

PRAYER

Lord, sometimes I feel that I'm alone. These waters I tread threaten to crest over me, pull me under, and cause me to drown in my sea of doubt. Thank you that you not only know the way to victorious living through your own experience, you walk with me each step of the way. I need only to hold your hand.

PART IV

ORDER

If only my memory were as long as my list.

Fortunate indeed, is the man who takes exactly the right measure of himself, and holds a just balance between what he can acquire and what he can use.

Source Unknown

Some days, even an umbrella won't keep you dry.

So do not worry, saying, 'What shall we eat?' or 'What shall we drink?' or 'What shall we wear?' For the pagans run after all these things, and your heavenly Father knows that you need them. But seek first his kingdom and his righteousness, and all these things will be given to you as *well.* (Matthew 6:31–33)

THE DAY SUPER MOM DIED

*Vivian believed in the Super Mom myth, and as a new mom, she strove for perfection. She boiled her baby's bibs, starched and ironed all his clothes, cooked and pureed his food, and changed him after every spit up. In addition to all of her baby's needs, Vivian made sure the rest of the family felt no neglect. Towels were never used twice. No dish was left on the counter unwashed. And she made sure Daddy had his favorite pie for dessert. She kept the house so immaculate *Better Homes and Gardens* could have done a photo shoot without an appointment.

When she was hospitalized from exhaustion, Vivian's physician lectured her. "It will do no harm if your children eat a little dirt once in a while. They might actually be a little healthier in the long run. Children don't need a sterile environment. But they do need a mother who is awake."

Vivian recovered and resumed her activities. While she remembered her doctor's words, she was not ready to abandon her goal to be Mom of the Century. She remained convinced there was a magic formula that would allow her to be the best mom, best wife, best worker, best daughter, and best homemaker in the world. *It's just a matter of proper balance,* she told herself.

Like Don Quixote of song, she pursued the Impossible Dream. With every magazine article and online housekeeping blog she read about successful women, she determined the windmills of perfection were just within reach. All she needed was to be a little more organized.

One day, her most esteemed colleague—a highly successful pediatrician— admitted she was inept when it came to homemaking. Vivian finally realized that perfection was an illusion. She began to bask in the sunshine of a child's smile rather than angst because her floors needed polishing.

The Rich Young Ruler met Jesus at night. He had it all—power, prestige, and wealth. Yet, he knew he lacked something. So, he asked the one who could fulfill this unnamed desire. The learned seeker was a good man who diligently followed the laws, "from his youth up," the Bible tells us.

We are told how puzzled he became when Jesus's advice was to sell all his property and follow him. Yet, this bright scholar, learned and able, could not humble himself to place God above what the world provided.

Vivian and the rich young man had earthly goals for which they labored. Both realized they came up wanting. The wealthy ruler went away, "sorrowful." Vivian traded her zeal and accepted God's better plan for her life. She testifies to how much richer her relationships, both professional and domestic, have become once she put God first. "Now my life seems more ordered than when I struggled to control everything."

The Lord wants the believer to place his relationship with the Father above all else—not out of jealousy for our attention. Rather, for the believer's benefit. He teaches us what is better and what is most worth pursuing. When we start and end each day with God, what falls in between is a little taste of Heaven and is sweeter than the darkest chocolate.

INSIGHT

Read 1 Peter 2:21, Psalm 37:23, Proverbs 4:12, and Jeremiah 10:23.

For what purpose has God called us? How does walking in Christ's steps provide a sense of freedom from ordering every aspect of our lives? Who will the Lord help order their steps? Why do you think delighting in the Lord makes life seem more organized? What does the Lord promise us if we order our steps according to his will? What do you think Jeremiah means when he warns that a person's steps are not their own? Does this knowledge change the way you plan your life? Have you ever experienced a time when God has disrupted your perfectly orchestrated life in order to bring you closer to him? God has promised to order the steps of those who delight in him.

PRAYER

Father, there are times when I feel I have no control at all and life is one mess after another. Other times, I'm afraid of losing the control I have. Help me to seek you first, and to trust you to order my steps wisely in order to bring me into a closer relationship with you.

He who washes floor while reading book makes soggy paper.

Neither circumcision nor uncircumcision means anything: what counts is a new creation. (Galatians 6:15)

GRANDMA PRAYED WHILE IRONING

"Did you have the oven on for a reason?" my husband asks.

I shrug my shoulders, stand the iron on its end, and shuffle to the kitchen to take the burnt cake out of the oven.

My husband is able to read the paper, watch television, work on the computer and carry on a conversation all at the same time. If I tried to do that, I'd start writing the script for a current police drama into my devotional manuscript and preach to the cat while I filled up his dish. My fragmented mind simply cannot assimilate multiple, simultaneous stimuli.

In true contradiction to my natural bents, my mantra is "Life is too short to wait for toast." Consequently, while the bread is in the toaster, I run water to rinse the dishes before putting them in the dishwasher. The stream from the faucet reminds me I need to wash the floor. I run to the pantry and grab my mop and set up to give the floor a good once over. However, I'm distracted by the finger smudges on the mirror. I leave the mopping to fetch the glass cleaner that is stored in the bathroom closet. On the way, I notice the laundry basket is filled to overflowing. I pick up the basket to take to the laundry room off the kitchen. That's when I trip over the mop I left propped against the counter and notice the sink has filled and flooded to the floor.

All because I wanted toast.

Whether we want to admit it or not, our spiritual lives are equally frazzled. We try to squeeze in a devotional while burping the baby. If we time things exactly right, we might be able to attend the women's night out if Grandma will pick up Hunter from his Boy Scout meeting. When we finally get to bed, we fall asleep saying exhausted prayers. With all the modern conveniences, shouldn't our lives be less complicated? Yet, we sadly realize that perhaps our forebears, who labored from dusk to dawn, had less anxiety than their modern counterparts. Our familial, societal, and religious obligations crowd our calendars to the point of near insanity.

My dear senior friend, Sally, who probably earned every one of her thick, gray curls, confided that she did her best praying while kneading her famous cinnamon rolls. "Maybe that's why everyone raves over them so," she said.

Lydia was a dealer in cloth. When she heard Paul preach, she gave her heart to Jesus, becoming the first convert in Macedonia. But, instead of selling her business to sit in the synagogue day and night, God used her talents to help spread the gospel. As she traded her purple cloths, she shared what the Lord had done in her life.

Perhaps the doing matters less to God than being in his presence. Yet, we Martha types still find sitting at the feet of Jesus more and more difficult. Rather than angst, burdened with guilt that we don't seem to have the time we'd like for Bible study, we would do well to remember God understands. He only asks to keep him involved with whatever we are doing. Prayer does not need to be on our knees 24/7. He hears us when we lift our hearts as we lift our laundry baskets. If the only time we can find to sing choruses is in the shower, that's okay. If we pray while waiting in the grocery store check-out line, that's okay, too. A heart that is tuned in to God wherever life takes her finds a God ready to listen.

INSIGHT

Read 1 Thessalonians 5:16-18, Psalm 5:3, 55:17, 88:1-2.

How do we balance the command to pray without ceasing with the demands of raising a family … especially working moms with active children? David's psalms convey an attitude of constant prayer. Yet, he was a king, his attention in high demand. He was a warrior, requiring his senses to be on high alert. Affairs of the nation were constantly on his mind … and many opposed him. He knew the decisions he made would affect the whole nation. Do you think he struggled to find time to pray? How do you think he managed to keep his philosophy of constant prayer?

PRAYER

Father, I do need you every minute of every day. Keep my heart tuned in to you whatever my task at the moment might be. May my heart be always ready to give you praise, even when I wipe up spilled milk.

The beauty of planning my day
is to find at the end of it
how different it was from
what I imagined at the beginning.

Many, Lord my God, are the wonders you have done, the things you planned for us. None can compare with you; were I to speak and tell of your deeds, they would be too many to declare. (Psalm 40:5)

A GOOD PLAN PLANS FOR CHANGE

Even the most disorganized person becomes befuddled when the unexpected intrudes into an otherwise organized day. Most of us follow some sort of predictable routine. Perhaps a walk at a particular time of day or a cup of coffee first thing in the morning. We become so engrossed with the process of living, we pay little attention to how programmed we are until something disrupts our day.

If I had checked my calendar, I'd have realized I had two meetings to attend—both scheduled at the same time. But, for some reason, I didn't. And I thought I had a free night. So my husband and I decided to make a date. Dinner, a movie, and time with my man proved to be an unexpected blessing. One I'd have missed if God had not erased my memory of less important matters. As if he said, "You need to spend more time in your marriage and less time away from it."

Our God is one of order. The physical world attests to it. We know that no two objects can occupy the same place at the same time without cataclysmic consequences. God, the author of order, is also a God of variety. He invented the seasons, the tides, and the cycles of the moon. While there are predictable patterns in the Universe, that same Universe changes constantly.

On his second missionary journey, Paul had a sudden change of plans. "When they came to the border of Mysia, they tried to enter Bithynia, but the Spirit of Jesus would not allow them to." (Acts 16.7) Paul entered into Macedonia, (Europe) preaching in Philippi and establishing an important church there.

When ships at sea veer off course, they need to adjust speed and direction. In order to return to the correct latitude and longitude, the rudder requires realignment. God knows our yesterdays and our tomorrows. He wants to keep us on course. Sometimes, he has to make changes in our plans so that he can fit us into his.

INSIGHT

Read Proverbs 19:21, Isaiah 29:15, James 4:13–16, 1 Peter 1:18–20.

Have you ever experienced an interruption in your plans where God has blessed you in unexpected ways? We cannot hide our agenda from God. He knows what we think we will do. When we are surrendered to him, he will guard us against destructive decisions and point us in more worthwhile directions. We can say with determination we will do this or that on any given day. Ultimately, God will direct our todays as well as our tomorrows. From before Creation, God had a plan to save mankind, and the whole of the Bible is God's design for that plan. Though men made war against him, God's will prevailed. Why should this be of comfort to us?

PRAYER

Lord, you know my ups and downs, my comings and goings. The Psalmist said there is nowhere we can hide from you. Help me to surrender my life, to place my todays and tomorrows in your loving care. Help me to see you first before I make my plans and to trust in you when those plans seem to go haywire.

If you reap what you sow, why is my garden full of weeds?

Sluggards do not plow in season; so at harvest time they look but find nothing. (Proverbs 20:4)

CONFESSIONS OF A GARDEN SLUGGARD

One day my mother stopped in unexpectedly and presented me with a beautiful azalea bush. I was pleasantly surprised. Two days later, she asked me to return it to her. "What was I thinking? You're lethal around plants."

Sadly, her condemnation was well earned. She remembered how I killed my daughter's ivy. I talked to it daily, fed it fertilizer, and watered it routinely. I begged it not to die. No use. The plant met its end in the dumpster like all its predecessors.

I love flowers. I would like to have an attractive flowerbed along the backyard. Sometimes, I even dream about velvety roses in the spring and how I would take my coffee out in the morning as they opened to meet the sun. However, the realities of my inadequacies shatter my visions. If the truth were known, I'm more highly adept with a golf club than a hoe. I must confess that I am the gardening sluggard who expects a bountiful harvest without the labor.

Most people erroneously equate the word sluggard with laziness. Rather than being slack, the sluggard expends energy at the wrong time doing the wrong things. The sluggard will plant seeds during an eroding rain and blame the squirrels when nothing grows.

The story is told of two monks who each planted a shrub. The first monk prayed for sun and rain. The shrub died. The second monk's shrub flourished. Disappointed in the outcome, the first monk asked the second monk what he did differently. The second monk told the first monk, "I, too, prayed for my shrub. But I asked God to give it what it needed." That is the difference between the sluggard's and the reaper's gardens. The reaper knows he is wanting and goes to the supplier. The sluggard foolishly tries to cultivate within his misinformation.

*Wendy believed if she gave her children everything they wanted, they would love her. Instead, she fostered weeds of greed and selfishness. One by one, her children ended up in the juvenile system, eventually graduating to hard core prisons. *Betty lacked much in financial resources, but she prayed daily for wisdom to raise her children. Each bloomed into productive members of society. In turn, these rigorous flowers nurtured Betty in her old age.

Likewise, without proper cultivation of the heart, the garden of our soul suffers. We try to live out our Christian experience in our limited knowledge. We follow a rigorous routine of Bible reading and prayer. Every time the church door opens, we're first in line for seating. Yet, all the exterior trappings of our religiosity bring no lasting peace or joy. We are as fruitless as the garden seeds sown out of season—and we wonder why.

Such was my estate. I tried to live my Christian life as I try to garden, vigorously applying haphazard and useless energy, which availed nothing. I lacked the indwelling of God's Holy Spirit. What I perceived as truth was nothing more than dead leaves raked from the wisdom of pastors, Sunday School Teachers, and acquaintances. My definition of Christian was based upon what others believed—a counterfeit faith that would never blossom. My heart was a spiritual dessert, arid and fruitless.

But when soil is in need of water, God will send the rain. He did so for me, and He'll do so for anyone who asks.

Then, and only then, will our spirit blossom as God intended.

INSIGHT

Read Isaiah 1:13, Isaiah 29:3, Hosea 10:12–13, Galatians 6:7–8, Romans 1:5.

What is the difference between ritual sacrifice and sacrifice from the heart? Why did the Lord institute sacrifices? From early Mosaic times, God sought to be honored through good deeds. Why would God be displeased with the very sacrifices he ordained to be done? How can we go through ritualistic Christian practices and yet our hearts be far from God? What sacrifices does God require rather than ritual ones? Why does God prefer obedience through faith rather than ritualistic good deeds? Why do they bring about a fruitless garden?

PRAYER

Lord, sometimes when I am in church or I read my Bible or go through the motions of good deeds, I am doing so because this is what I think I should do. My body is in motion while my mind is focused on other, less important things. I ask forgiveness when my acts are done without thought, without heart, or from external efforts rather than a desire from within. I ask for a Spirit-indwelling that will spur me to desire to do good rather than sowing good deeds that bring no fruit.

If wishing made it so, I'd be wearing a size eight and driving a Mercedes.

Take delight in the LORD, and he will give you the
desires of your heart. (Psalm 37:4)

SHOULD OR WANT?

I know the drill. I hear it from my doctor with every visit. Lose weight, eat morenutritiously, and get more exercise. I know there are certain practices that need to change for optimal good health.

I vow to decrease my caffeine intake while increasing my fiber. I know I need to lose thirty pounds or more, complete thirty minutes of daily aerobic activity, drink eight glasses of water, and consume the requisite servings of fruits and vegetables.

With good intentions, I dust off the treadmill, put motivational stickers around the house, and keep a diary of my new healthy ambitions. In spite of determination, my bad habits resurface. "I just don't have enough will power," I moan while pouring my fourth cup ofcoffee.

Is my inability to change due to lack of motivation? Am I too weak of spirit? "Why," I reprimand myself, "can't you change?"

Perhaps it is because I suffer from the *shoulds*. I should drink less caffeine. I *should* exercise more. I should lose weight. Every magazine I pick up has more than half of its content devoted to the *shoulds*.

I don't comply because I lack the *wants*. Oh, it's true I'd like to be as beautiful as Anne Hathaway, as athletic as Jessica Biel, and as perky as Reese Witherspoon, but am I willing to make the sacrifice to obtain these characteristics? Do I have the commitment for change? Sadly, no.

When *Susy Baker discovered her daughter's constant ear infections were the result of exposure to second-hand cigarette smoke, she evaluated what was more important—her habit or her daughter's health. Convicted that a behavior change was needed to protect her daughter, her motivations changed. With a higher desire, she made the commitment to take the cigarette smoke outside. Eventually, she quit smoking entirely. When her *should* became a *want,* she was finally able to rearrange her priorities.

Parenting requires a spirit of want rather than should. We know we should model good behavior for our children. Not until we come to a place where desire exceeds contemplation will our positive role-modeling become true, not contrived. Our children will know the difference between what we say and what we do and if our hearts are in what we do.

What of our spiritual lifestyles? We believe we *should* read the Bible more, attend church regularly, and give generously. Every devotional article we read reminds us of the benefits when we do these things. Yet, our striving toward these goals wanes as the mundane erodes our best intentions.

God does not desire the empty exercise of religiosity. He wants a heart that desires him. The more we seek him, the more we want to be in his presence. We no longer pray because we *should*. We pray because our day is incomplete without spending time alone with Him.

INSIGHT

Read Psalm 145:16, Isaiah 26:9, Luke 6:21a, 1 Peter 2:2, Proverbs 19:2, Isaiah 57:10.

Why is knowledge without desire useless? Why does God say that our relationship with him must be based on desire rather than duty? Which does God prefer … a heart burdened with guilt from infrequent prayer and Bible reading or a heart that desires to feed on God's presence and his word? If we feel we lack desire, how do we stimulate that desire? Desire cannot be manufactured. God himself will draw us to him, if we ask him.

PRAYER

Lord, the familiar chorus says that you are our one desire. Sometimes, I feel so far away from you. I know I should spend daily time in your word. When I make myself do so, often my thoughts wander, and my heart feels far away from you. Infuse me, Lord, to desire a deeper relationship with you. Fill me with your presence. Then, like your servant, David, I will be glad when I go into the house of the Lord.

PART V

PROTECT

I enlisted for matrimony but was drafted for motherhood.

To secure peace is to prepare for war.

Karl (Carl) von Clausewitz,
(1780–1831)
Russian general and military strategist

We need encouragement the most
when we have failed the worst.

Praise be to the God and Father of our Lord Jesus Christ, the Father of compassion and the God of all comfort. (2 Corinthians 1:3)

ROOT FOR THE HOME TEAM

The audience fell silent as the two finalists held one another's hand and waited breathlessly for the judges' decision. Who would be the next Miss County Teenager?

The name of the first runner up was called, and she graciously took her place with the other contestants. She watched jealously as the winner was crowned. When all the pictures and interviews were finished and the audience had departed, the girl asked her mother if she could stop for an ice cream cone on the way home.

While clasping her second-place trophy, the mother yanked the girl by the arm, pulled her from the auditorium and screamed, "Why should I? You didn't win!" The girl bowed her head in shame—not because she lost, but because she had disappointed her mother.

Another contestant in the pageant was not even a finalist. Her mother ran up to her and gave her a hug. "I'm so proud of you," the mother said. "That was one of the most difficult things you've ever done. You managed it with dignity and grace. You are a winner in my book. Let's get a pizza and celebrate."

The first girl never entered another pageant. The second girl continued on to obtain a crown in a local contest. She never became Miss America, nor did she walk among the stars. She became a wife and mother. In later years, she expressed gratitude for the pageant experiences that taught her many useful skills. Most importantly, she is grateful to a mother who encouraged her even when she lost.

In our Christian walk, we stumble and fall … so many times we lose count. God does not desire for us to hang our head in shame, nor does he delight in punishing us when we fall short of our own expectations. Instead, he is like the second mother. He wraps us in his loving arms and congratulates our best efforts. He instructs us in the ways we can go to avoid bruises and pain in the future. He is our constant cheerleader and surrounds us with a chorus of angels. His word is filled with phrases such as "be not afraid, be strong and of good courage, and the Lord your God is with you." He loves us even in our imperfection.

He picks us up from the dust and washes off the dirt. Full of love, he looks into our eyes, telling us that he has done it all for us already. All we need to do is be faithful, and we will win the prize—eternity with God.

INSIGHT

Read 1 John 2:1, John 14:26, 2 Chronicles 20:15, Philippians 3:13–15, Philippians 4:13, Genesis 32:24–28.

How long should we keep trying to right a wrong or accomplish a task before we give up? When should we surrender to fear? Has anyone come by your side as a cheerleader? What impact did that have for you? How has God encouraged you lately? How can we be cheerleaders for our children? Jacob was rebellious from birth. He deceived and connived. He was also taken advantage of by his father-in-law. Yet, God continued to bless him and encourage him throughout his struggles … those of his own making and those resulting from others' actions.

PRAYER

Lord, I have fallen down so many times, yet you come whenever I ask to pick me up and set me straight. You do not chastise me for failing when I sincerely try. Thank you for walking beside me each step of my journey, for being my cheerleader, and reminding me that I can do all things through you.

Sticks and stones break bones.
Harsh words crush the spirit.

Anxiety weighs down the heart, but a kind word cheers it up. (Proverbs 12:25)

LOVE IN A SUITCASE

*Janelle wept because of Rachel's disobedience. Janelle had exhausted every parenting trick in the book. Yet, the more she punished her daughter, the worse her behavior became. Pleas and recriminations fell on deaf ears. Janelle prayed the prayer of the battle fatigued, asking for God's intercession.

When Rachel readied to travel on a ski trip with her classmates, Janelle felt squeezed. If she allowed the teenager to go, wouldn't it seem Rachel had been rewarded for poor behavior? After much prayer, Janelle decided to allow Rachel to fulfill her plans. With no fanfare, the fearful mom slipped a note inside Rachel's suitcase:

> My dearest daughter,
>
> I know you are troubled right now. I know that you and I have had a lot of arguments lately. You are probably afraid—afraid of growing up and going on your own. I just want you to know that I believe in you. I know that you are going to be just fine. You will become a wonderful woman, wife, and mother.
>
> I want you to know that no matter how mad you are at me, you will never destroy my love for you. You will always be my daughter whom I love.
>
> Mom

When Rachel returned, she said nothing regarding her mother's note. But her behavior improved from the moment she walked in the door. Rachel had been changed by an unbreakable love, a love that had withstood her best efforts to destroy it. When she felt the least deserving, affirmation was what she needed most.

Sometimes God sends us blessings when we feel the least deserving. "But God demonstrates his own love for us in this: While we were still sinners, Christ died for us." (Romans 5:8).

God's love is not dependent upon our actions. It is given freely without condition. And when we realize this, we are changed by his steadfast commitment to us, one that transcends our rebelliousness.

INSIGHT

Read Jeremiah 31:3, John 1:16–17, Ephesians 2:1–4, I Timothy 1:14, Psalm 84:11, Romans 9:16, Ephesians 1:6, Ezekiel 16:20, Isaiah 54:10.

God promises, from the oldest interactions with his creation, to love his people unconditionally. Even when they turn from him. His love can never be deterred. Yes … we see that sometimes he must be severe in his discipline. That does not diminish his unconditional love. As God has loved us unconditionally, we are able to extend that same love to our children with his help and wisdom.

PRAYER

Lord, I thank you for your unbreakable love towards me … even when I resist you. Infuse me with this same dogged love for those whom you have placed in my care.

No conventional weapon fashioned by man has yet stood against a parent who fights for their child.

Whoever fears the LORD has a secure fortress, and for their children it will be a refuge. (Proverbs 14:26)

BATTLE FATIGUES

In every civilization, the soldier was sent into battle with certain rudimentary protective garb. Whether it is the Roman with feathered helmet or desert fatigues of the Mideast conflicts, the soldier in combat is dressed in full regalia for the job. Likewise, parents need protection in the war to steel their sanity.

The Belt of Truth: When a soldier is called to attention, he tucks in the tummy and stands ready. In the same way, God wants us to take his truth and wrap it around us. This truth is that Jesus is God's son—crucified for our sins, buried, risen and who now is at the right hand of the Father. Furthermore, Jesus has already won the war.

The Breastplate of Righteousness: Satan wants us to believe we are too sinful to be forgiven or that we are not in need of forgiveness. It is incomprehensible that a Holy God would choose to sacrifice his sinless son on a cross for an undeserving and unappreciative world. But that was exactly what he did. This breastplate that guards our hearts, the seat of our vulnerability, is the promise of eternal life when we accept the gift God freely offers.

Shoes of the Gospel of Peace: The enemy hurls doubt to unsettle the peace God gives. When our spouse is late, the enemy will seed distrust in our hearts. Or perhaps our spirits are wounded by an unkind word. Without claiming God's peace, the hurt will fester and infect our relationships. But God's peace is ours to claim.

Shield of Faith: It is difficult to feel spiritual after scooping up dog poop and laundering vomit-laced sheets. It is difficult to pray when the baby has been crying all night from teething. It is difficult to recognize the Holy Spirit's work in our lives when Katie comes home with failing grades. The enemy attacks when we are the most exhausted. As God's child, we are heir to all of Heaven's power. With this confidence, we can boldly stand regardless of our circumstances.

Helmet of Salvation: Satan wants the believer to drown in meaningless stimuli. By intruding into our prayers and preventing our spiritual edification, he fills our minds with trash. He wants to cut us off from Christ's holy influence. We serve him because his very nature is alive within us.

Sword of the Spirit: God has given us his own presence in the form of the Holy Spirit. When Jesus ascended into Heaven, he reassured his followers that nothing could sever us from him. Satan has no dominion over us and must surrender in the face of this Holy Ghost power.

Armed with such an arsenal, the muddy footprints no longer seem like a personal vendetta. Instead, God fills us with the knowledge of blessings the source of the footprints brings.

INSIGHT

Read Ephesians 6:10–18, Deuteronomy 20:1, and 2 Samuel 22:35.

What pieces of armor does Paul list? Why these? What additional instructions does he give to add to our armament? Why does the believer need to be ready for battle at all times? Do we sometimes feel we fight our battles alone? Remember Gideon? He whittled a large army down to a few yet defeated the enemy because the Lord was on his side. Numbers do not matter to the Lord. He is all the power and strength we need, and he will equip us to wage whatever war we need in the enemy's fight against our families.

PRAYER

Father God, help me to establish myself as a warrior mom. I realize the battle begins on my knees. Help me to remember you are always at my side, though ten thousand are poised against me.

Fear not the bee. Fear only his sting.

Though an army besiege me, my heart will not fear; though war break out against me, even then will I be confident. (Psalm 27:3)

BATTLE WITH A BUMBLEBEE

As a single mother, I was the children's sole protector. The job of bodyguard seemed a bit overwhelming at times. So when the little ones were safely tucked into bed for the night, I occasionally allowed myself the luxury of a lengthy bubble bath. The long hard day seemed to melt away with the steam.

One night while enjoying this occasional privilege, I heard a familiar humming sound. Then I spied the enemy, a gigantic bumblebee. With the exception of spiders, snakes, and bees, I am not easily intimidated. As a little girl, I was stung badly, and the memory lingered through adulthood. Just the *buzz* will throw me into a state of panic.

The bee hovered over my bathwater and blocked my exit, keeping me a prisoner. As I pondered a safe exit, the sound of a crying baby made my heart sputter. No matter how fearsome this enemy, my child needed me. With my towel as a sword, I waged war against the mighty bee, smiling victoriously when its carcass hit the floor. I threw on my robe and hugged my baby, glad when his wails turned into giggles.

Parenting is not for the fainthearted. We are besieged in every direction with our worst fears. Will we ever get those brownies made and be on time for work? We sigh with relief when the children climb on the school bus, then turn around and find the lunch pails lined up on the counter. These aggravations pale in comparison to the sleepless nights fighting fevers and waiting for prom attendees to return home.

And we worry because Janie's boyfriend rides too close to the wild side for our liking. We choke on our fright during broken bones from football games and sprained wrists from cheerleading routines. Our children are vulnerable, and the weight of responsibility presses upon us. Every decision we make on their behalf impacts their future.

God promised He would stand on our right side and our left. He has vowed to be our shield against any arrow the enemy hurls our way. Within that knowledge, our fears subside. We are free to battle with confidence.

INSIGHT

Read Psalm 35:1, Psalm 139:17–18, Ephesians 6:12, 1 Timothy 6:11–12, 1 Peter 5:8.

According to Paul, with whom do we wrestle? Do you think these spirits sometimes manifest themselves in physical situations? God is our salvation against our enemies … especially those that come at us unaware. Scripture also reminds us that we should be diligent and "on guard" against the devil's wiles. Yet, we are assured that God fights for us. We do not need to succumb to anxious thoughts for God is ever present. We should not be afraid to fight the good fight of faith. We can stand firm, knowing that no matter our situation, someone somewhere has experienced these same problems. We are not alone. Wrap up that towel and swat away.

PRAYER

Lord, sometimes my heart skips a beat when I receive bad or difficult news. Am I sufficiently prepared to win this war? Help me to remember that you go behind, ahead, and beside me in every situation.

A mom's first aid kit contains kisses to be amply applied on the forehead.

So do not fear, for I am with you; do not be dismayed, for I am your God. I will strengthen you and help you; I will uphold you with my righteous right hand. (Isaiah 41:10)

STRANDED BUT NOT FORGOTTEN

Parents spend large portions of their day rescuing their charges from precarious situations. Sometimes our children wander too far into deep water. Too often, their predicaments are the result of foolish indiscretions.

At age three, my son loved to climb. He found a fence ledge that became higher as it trailed along a hill. He hopped up on the short end of the ledge. Before I could reach him, he'd inched along to a point ten feet off the ground. When he looked down, fear replaced his former bravery. He screamed for assistance. As he was too far from my grasp, I encouraged him, step by step, to inch his way back to where he could safely fall into my arms. I hugged him, kissed him on the cheek, and told him to never climb that ledge again. He nodded agreement while tears rolled down his flushed cheeks.

The older the child, the greater possibility their problems may grow beyond immediate solvability. We are painfully aware that those magic curative kisses are insufficient to heal our teenage daughter's broken heart. More than ever before, we need to relinquish their care to the watchful eye of the Lord of Lords. Surrender is painful.

As a synagogue leader, Jairus was familiar with the Scriptures. He was ready with perfectly padded answers to the perplexities of life. But when his beloved daughter fell gravely ill, his prefabricated solutions seemed like empty words. Needing something better, Jairus sought the Messiah. He found Jesus surrounded by clamoring needs, only to be told his daughter was already dead. There was no point in disturbing the Master.

With compassion, Jesus told Jairus, "Don't be afraid; just believe" (Mark 5:36). Jairus returned with Jesus and a selected few of the disciples. Jesus breathed life into the girl. She arose immediately and was given food to eat. Things were back to normal. All his wealth, knowledge, and power could not save his daughter. His only hope had been in a poor, obscure carpenter. Jesus sees when our children are out of our protective watch, when our frail kisses are useless. Our Warrior Savior shields them when our arms are too short.

INSIGHT

Read Numbers 111:23, 2 Corinthians 12:9, 2 Corinthians 3:4–6, Jeremiah 32:27,

Psalm 16:5–8, Isaiah 59:11, Philippians 4:14.

Are you facing a crisis or situation in your life, or your family's life, that you feel is beyond your capability to solve? When we think of the word sufficient in our English language, we often think of "just enough." However, the word translated as sufficient in Scripture, or its root sufficiency, actually means "more than enough." Our God is all-sufficient. His arm of deliverance is long and strong. Always there when we need his wisdom, grace, and strength. We can do all things because he has promised to give us the strength to do those things he calls us to do … including our parenting.

PRAYER

Father God, you know my frame. You know my weaknesses. You know my fears. My child is past the place where a simple kiss can make any booboo disappear. How can I protect this little life from a world that is bent toward hostility, anger, and selfishness? Help me to trust you more. To lean on your wisdom and strength, when mine is gone.

PART VI

SERVE

**I might be built like the Pillsbury Doughboy,
but that doesn't mean I know how to cook.**

Love is a fruit in season at all times, and in reach of every hand.
Mother Teresa

Love, like salt, makes even burnt potatoes taste good.

Here I am! I stand at the door and knock. If anyone hears my voice and opens the door, I will come in and eat with that person, and they with me. (Revelation 3:20)

PASS THE LOVE, PLEASE

Cain, a tiller of the soil, and Abel, a shepherd, both made sacrifices to God. The Bible tells us that God favored Abel's offering, that of the lamb. Rejected, Cain's hatred toward Abel stewed, and he killed his brother in a jealous rage. We are not told what was wrong with Cain's offering, but we do know that Abel's sacrifice was considered better because it was given "by faith" (Hebrews 11:4). Perhaps Cain's fruit was damaged or imperfect, or perhaps the poison in his heart spoiled his offering. What matters most to God is not what is on the menu, but how we put it on the plate.

Some people say that hunger makes the best seasoning. According to my mother, everything tastes better made with love. It doesn't matter whether the main course is flung on the barbecue, broiled in the oven, or delivered at the door. When love is added, the meal is sure to please.

My husband is now our primary cook. He enjoys garnering recipes from the internet. Like Emeril Lagasse, a famous cook in years past ... the "pork fat rules" mogul ... my husband will "bam" even his scrambled eggs to bring them "up a notch." My scrambled eggs, however, look like something out of a Dr. Seuss book.

Whether dinner consists of Chicken-in-the-Box or First Prize Blooper of the Month Casserole, as long as the main course is served in an atmosphere of love, you'll win the blue ribbon for family appreciation. For even the most delicately prepared salmon will curl if eaten in sour company. Love, no matter how it is served up, always tastes good. It satiates the soul.

Like a soggy tuna sandwich on crusty bread, our souls are dissatisfied. We crave flavor in our lives. But what we truly lack to spice up our existence is Love—the healing Love found in Jesus Christ, God's offering for humankind. We push him away because we believe he wants to spoil our fun. So we eat alone, and our stomachs growl with unrelenting hunger.

Our Savior, like a freshly brewed cup of coffee, is rich in aroma, full of flavor, and warms the soul through and through. He wants to sit and feast at our table. When He breaks bread with us, he fills us to capacity. We will never hunger again. He will not come, however, unless we open the door. Will you let him in?

INSIGHT

Read Job 10:12, Psalm 90:14, Psalm 63:3, John 13:1, Ephesians 1:4–5, 1 John 3:1–3.

From these Scriptures, how is God's love defined? Through the Lord's love, we are adopted and are heirs together with Christ. So, because of his redemptive love, we can now be called the Children of God. We who are earthly know how to love our children. How much more has the father lavished his love on us?

PRAYER

Lord, I cannot fathom the depth of your love for me … one who is undeserving, yet you gave everything to save me from sin's power. Help me to love my children with the same love you have given me … unconditionally, thoroughly, protectively, and compassionately.

A cat will be your friend as long as you have tuna juice on your apron.

Greater love has no one than this: to lay down one's life for one's friends. (John 15:13)

FRIENDSHIP IS STICKY BUSINESS

While shared activities may be useful in establishing close ties with our children, a friend is more than a costumed playmate. Webster defines *friend* as "one who is attached to another by affection." Attachment denotes a joining that is not easily separated.

Friendship is about the presence of self. It has to do with occupying the same space and time, whether with laughter or tears. The activity itself is not the crucial element. A child wants to know a parent is near—not from a sense of duty—but from choice.

Friendship is more about the being than the doing. It is not about how cleverly we read or the ingenuity we display during game time. Nor is friendship about who wins the *Sorry* tournament.

A true friend is like adhesive. One who does not let go. A friend is someone whom we admire and respect. A friend sets an example, someone we wish we could be more like. A friend stays the course no matter what storms may threaten the venture. A true friend does not criticize. Rather a friend encourages. A friend does not foster discouragement. Instead, a friend motivates.

A friend never yells. A friend's words of correction are like music to the ear.

A friend postpones discipline in order to listen. A friend stays by your side until you fall asleep. A friend walks with you even though his feet are sore. A friend trudges through five-foot snowdrifts to bring you chicken soup. A friend runs the race beside you and cries out, "You can do it."

A friend hears, "I love you," when we yell, "I hate you."

Instead of pointing out your faults, a friend lists your strengths. A friend helps you pack for the big trip. And most of all, a friend knows when to hold you tight and when to give you space.

Christ is a friend like no other. He has shown his affection for us through his sacrifice on the cross. He desires to be in our presence day by day. He accepts us as we are. He wants us to cry out to him when the lights go out and no candle can be found. He comforts us when the very act of getting out of bed drains our last ounce of energy. He weeps with us when we are sad, and he laughs with us when we are joyful. He knows when to walk beside us or carry us the rest of the way.

With a friend like him, we need no other.

INSIGHT

Read the account of David's friendship with Jonathan: 1 Samuel 18:1–4, 19:1–6, 20:17, 41; 23:18. See also Isaiah 41:8, Proverbs 18:24, and John 15:15.

How did Jonathan show sacrificial love toward his friend, David? How does Christ demonstrate his friendship toward us?

PRAYER

Lord, I thank you that you are my friend, that you stick to me no matter what, through storms and through sunshine. Give me a heart that is grateful. Help me to stop complaining and remember your vast and wonderful love to me. Teach me how to be friends with my children, to enjoy them, to laugh with them, to play with them, and learn from them.

Some days, life seems like a Lego tile—bumpy on the outside and all stuck underneath.

"Now I commit you to God and to the word of his grace, which can build you up and give you an inheritance among all those who are sanctified." (Acts 20:32)

UPON THIS ROCK, I WILL BUILD MY FUTURE

The storm finally quieted. The little girl held her mother's hand as the family drove through town to survey the damage. They came upon a flattened house. The girl cocked her head as she scanned the ruins. Then, full of understanding, she told her mother, "Uh-oh! They didn't build their house on the Rock."

In the Gospel of Matthew, Jesus told the story of two builders and two foundations. When the rains buffeted, the house on the rock withstood the storm. The man who built his home on sand found nothing but ruin after the rains (Matthew 7:24-27).

But how do you construct a sure foundation when the ground is carpeted with Transformers?

The answer is—one broken toy at a time.

A building project requires wisdom, fortitude, and patience. Competent engineers develop a blueprint and stick to the design. We wonder how anything resembling a home will arise from the pile of boards and cement bags. The skilled carpenter places his tools strategically about the worksite— yet, to the casual observer, havoc appears to reign. Construction is messy, and the ultimate test of endurance. But when the spiral staircase becomes a reality, we rejoice at the sight of the long-awaited prize.

Then, and only then, do we appreciate the wait.

In many ways parenting is like building a house. We want our children to grow up to be productive adults. We know that the end product will require all the patient molding of an artisan. We are weary and worried that our best efforts will be like sand.

Long ago, before the foundation of the world, our loving Father looked down the path of history. He saw a world in chaos and in a hopeless state. He saw you and me in the mass of confusion. He had a blueprint for the world. His master plan was to send his only Son to die on the cross for the redemption of humankind.

What we sometimes fail to remember is that God planned our lives before we even lived a single day. He has more knowledge of how our house will look than we could ever have imagined. When we feel we are being tugged like silly putty, we can be confident that God is shaping us into his pride and joy.

INSIGHT

Read Matthew 7:24–26, Luke 6:46–49, Acts 4:8–12, Matthew 16:13–19, Isaiah 28:16.

That the parable of the house on the rock and the house on the sand are in two gospels is significant. To whom was Jesus preaching? Jesus was a carpenter and understood the importance of a solid foundation. When Jesus asked the disciples what the population in general thought him to be, the disciples simply reported the standard rumors. Then Jesus asked, "Who do you think I am?" Peter, the brash fisherman, quickly responded. What did he say? What did Jesus mean that "upon this" he'd build his church? To what was Isaiah referring to when he mentioned the foundation that would never be shaken? Have you laid your heart upon the sure foundation of Christ?

PRAYER

Lord, you are my rock, my sure foundation. I lay my life and my purpose upon you.

Whoever said marriage was all about compromise never had a joint checking account.

Submit to one another out of reverence to Christ.
(Ephesians 5:21)

THE FIFTY-FIFTY CONUNDRUM

"Marriage is not fifty-fifty," I heard Dr. Phil announce on national television. "It's one-hundred and one-hundred."

When did Dr. Phil steal my idea? Of course, the concept was not mine alone. God's wisdom is rarely unique to one individual.

I thought back to an office bridal shower several years ago. The gifts had been opened and the cake served. Tom hurled jokes meant in fun but left the bride-to-be quivering in her boots. Others gave unsolicited advice about the merits of compromise. "After all," Sally said, "Marriage is a fifty-fifty proposition."

Like Job's Elihu, my silence ended.

"I disagree," I rebutted as a hundred pair of accusatory eyes trained in my direction. The blushing bride had an inquiring mind. "I'd like to know what you think."

"I don't believe in the fifty-fifty rule. I believe in the hundred-hundred rule," I said. Everyone merely assumed I had failed math. "That's impossible," Orlando quipped.

I tried to explain. "The fifty-fifty rule leads to scorekeeping. The husband thinks that since he sat through that boring romance movie, she should go with him to the monster truck rally. The wife thinks that because she spent the whole day cleaning the house, he should take her out to dinner."

"Well, that sounds reasonable," Eileen piped up.

This crowd would be difficult to convince. "The requests are valid but are spoken from selfish interests. On the surface, they seem fair and equitable."

"Why wouldn't they be?" Janice asked.

I smiled. "Because somebody always has to sacrifice. Not so, with the hundred-hundred principle.

The bride-to-be asked, "How does it work, then?"

I explained. "In the hundred-hundred formula, instead of distasteful tradeoffs, all decisions are based upon what is best for the marriage. When the marriage wins, everyone wins."

The bride-to-be squished her face in contemplation. "Sounds like a good plan," she said and scurried off to examine her treasures.

I don't know how this newlywed couple fared, for she left our workplace in search of bigger paychecks. But I do know that the formula works for all relationships, including those with our children. It is the formula God uses for us. His sole purpose is our ultimate well-being. How can you not love a God like that?

INSIGHT

Read Deuteronomy 5:4–5, Exodus 20:3, Deuteronomy 6:4–5, Mark 12:28–30, 1 Peter 3:1–7, Ephesians 5:21–31, Ephesians 6:1–9.

Some of these verses expand the commandments in Deuteronomy and Exodus toward familial, work, and community relationships. How does the command to love the Lord your God with all your heart fulfill the commands regarding our relationships? Paul cautions parents to not provoke their children to wrath. In what ways could we do that? How do we avoid doing so? How does the 100-100 principle help us in our parenting?

PRAYER

Lord, I want to place you first in my life. If I love you with all my heart, then your place in my life will be paramount. As I love you wholeheartedly, so will I love those in my life wholeheartedly with a love that only you can place in my heart. Let my love to my spouse, my children, my family, my neighbors, and my coworkers be an extension of your love to me.

I don't want fame or fortune—just an occasional pat on the back and a cup of coffee in the morning.

"Many women do noble things, but you surpass them all." Charm is deceptive, and beauty is fleeting; but a woman who fears the Lord is to be praised (Proverbs 31:29–30)

CELEBRATE YOUR FEMININITY

When every day is spent with cooking, diapering, cleaning, diapering, laundry, diapering, and more diapering, we easily forget that we are, above all else, women. Moms are daughters, wives, workers, church officers, and community volunteers in addition to being chauffeurs, nurses, maids, cooks, and waitresses. In spite of our various parts, the whole of who we are is a woman.

We have learned from our foremothers that femininity is not equated with subjugation. In our American culture, women have found nearly equal footing with men. Even so, we still want boys to be boys and girls to be girls. Just as God designed physical differences for the survival of the species, he has designed intrinsic differences for the betterment of a relationship. **The Woman of Noble Character** as described in Proverbs exemplifies that distinctiveness.

First of all, she is **competent.** Her husband is confident in her abilities. Whether she is a stay-at-home mom, an entrepreneur mom, or a work-for-hire-mom, her spouse and children rest in the knowledge that the house will still be standing when they come home, food will be in the refrigerator, and cookies will be ready for the Valentine's party at school. Sometimes Dad takes up the slack. Most times, Mom wants to make sure these things are accomplished.

The Woman of Noble Character knows how to manage her day. She is **organized** in her thought life. I imagine the night before, she has prepared for the next day's needs. Perhaps she has laid out the children's clothes or prepared the frozen orange juice for breakfast. In our current culture, sometimes working moms leave messages or call home to remind the helper to take care of these things. Perhaps, because for most moms these necessities are ingrained in the heart.

Thirdly, the Woman of Noble Character **prioritizes** her tasks. Her first thoughts are for her family and their needs. She also cares for her **community.**

For modern women, this might be her coworkers or staff, her church, or her garden club. She serves in these capacities, not to fill a void or to find the meaning of life. Her involvement is an extension of her already fulfilled life.

Most importantly, the Woman of Noble Character is **content** for she has found her purpose and identity. Her husband and children offer praises to her name. What higher accolade?

And what of those, like me, who can only dream of this woman's merit? My cooking, cleaning, and checkbook balancing skills are horrifically deficient. I am useless with a hoe. I leave my grocery lists on the table and sew buttons on cockeyed. I am rarely up before daylight and would rather tear up the putting green than remodel the living room. Do these deficiencies make me less feminine? I don't think so.

To be a woman fulfilled is to choose to be a servant. Whether she is career-driven or a home engineer, a woman's service is a natural extension of her femininity. All humankind has been created in the image of God (Genesis 1). As mirrors of God, he desires his creation to adopt the example of Christ: "Who, being in very nature[God, did not consider equality with God something to be used to his own advantage; rather, he made himself nothing by taking the very nature of a servant, being made in human likeness. And being found in appearance as a man, he humbled himself by becoming obedient to death—even death on a cross! who, being God himself, submitted to death—the ultimate servant. (Philippians 2:5-8)

In our roles as God's daughters and Christ's sisters, we celebrate our true femininity.

INSIGHT

Read Proverbs 31, Philippians 2:5–8, Matthew 25:13–28, Luke 19:11–27, 2 Corinthians 9:6–8, Ecclesiastes 11:6, Proverbs 13:4.

Paul reminds us that our labor, i.e., our parenting efforts, should model the servitude of Christ. Scripture promises fruit for our service—labors that are rooted in God's word and a heart that is in tune with the Lord's leading. What reassurances are found in the above verses? Note in the references to Jesus's story of the talents, some were given more than others. As parents we may not have abundant resources in our parenting quest. Yet, the Lord will multiply what we do have if surrendered to him.

PRAYER

Lord, give me a servant's heart. Help me to love as you have loved me. Help me to understand, my quest for patience is rooted in your divine instruction. Thank you for the privilege of being a parent. As I continue this thing called parenting, may I always be mindful that these gifts you have placed in my charge are ever present reminders of what it means to be your child.

> A handful of patience is worth more
> than a bushel of brains.
>
> A Danish Proverb

Thanks for taking the time to read *I Prayed for Patience: God Gave Me Children*. We hope you enjoyed the book. Your review comments are appreciated.

The author is available to speak at your women's events. Contact her through her website: www.lindarondeau.com or lindarondeau@gmail.com

ABOUT THE AUTHOR

The author of the acclaimed Hosea's Heart and Miracle on Maple Street, LINDA WOOD RONDEAU, a veteran social worker, writes from the heart of personal experience. Her blog, *Snark and Sensibility*, embodies her sense of humor, a trait she believes God gives parents for survival. A resident of Hagerstown, Maryland, the author shares her days with her husband and best friend in life, Steve. Readers may visit her website at www.lindarondeau.com. Contact the author on Facebook, Twitter, or Instagram.

OTHER BOOKS BY LINDA WOOD RONDEAU

Fiddlers Fling
Miracle on Maple Street
Snow on Bald Mountain
Hosea's Heart
The Fifteenth Article

Coming soon:
For the Love of Gib
It Really Is a Wonderful Life

43665922R00091

Made in the USA
Middletown, DE
27 April 2019